A Ticket to
Argentina

Suzanne Paul Dell'Oro

Carolrhoda Books, Inc. / Minneapolis

Photo Acknowledgments

Photographs, maps, and artworks are used courtesy of: John Erste, pp. 1, 2–3, 9, 12–13, 19, 23, 32–33, 39, 42–43; Laura Westlund, p. 4, 7; © TRIP/D. Saunders, pp. 4–5; © SuperStock, pp. 6 (left), 10; © M. Joly/D. Donne Bryant Stock, p. 6 (center); © Fritz Pölking/Visuals Unlimited, p. 6 (right); © Robert Fried, pp. 7, 12, 13 (both), 16 (left), 18, 22, 24, 28, 29 (left), 31 (both), 35 (left); © Roberto Bunge/D. Donne Bryant Stock, pp. 8, 35 (top right); © C. Goldin/D. Donne Bryant Stock, pp. 9 (left), 16 (center and right), 21 (top), 23 (top), 29 (right), 32, 35 (bottom), 39, 42, 44, 45; © Jean S. Buldain, p. 9 (right); UPI/Corbis-Bettmann, p. 11 (bottom); © Schulte/D. Donne Bryant Stock, pp. 14, 40 (bottom); © Victor Englebert, p. 15 (left); © TRIP/J. Drew, p. 15 (right); Hugo Dell'Oro, pp. 17, 20, 25, 43; © TRIP/M. Barlow, pp. 19, 41; © Charles W. McRae/Visuals Unlimited, pp. 23 (bottom), 33 (bottom); © William Banaszewski/Visuals Unlimited, p. 26 (left); Reuters/Wilson Malo/Archive Photos, p. 26 (right); © Mary & Lloyd McCarthy/Root Resources, pp. 27 (top), 30 (left); Press Association/Archive Photos, p. 27 (bottom); © M. Long/Visuals Unlimited, p. 29 (center); © R. Sanguinetti/D. Donne Bryant Stock, p. 30 (right); © Michel Gotin, p. 33 (top); © Max & Bea Hunn/SuperStock, p. 34; © Michael Moody/D. Donne Bryant Stock, p. 36; painting by Florencio Molina Campos, p. 37 (top); © Mrs. Jane H. Kriete/Root Resources, p. 37 (bottom); © Allan A. Philiba, p. 38; © TRIP/A. Ghazzal, p. 40 (top). Cover photo of Argentine girl and boy © Robert Fried.

Carolrhoda Books, Inc.
c/o The Lerner Publishing Group
241 First Avenue North
Minneapolis, Minnesota 55401 U.S.A.

Website address: www.lernerbooks.com

Library of Congress Cataloging-in-Publication Data

Dell'Oro, Suzanne Paul.
Argentina / by Suzanne Paul Dell'Oro.
    p. cm. — (A ticket to—)
    Includes index.
    Summary: Discusses the people, geography, religion, language, customs, lifestyle, and culture of Argentina.
    ISBN 1–57505–139–7 (lib. bdg. : alk. paper)
    1. Argentina—Juvenile literature. [1. Argentina.] I. Title. II. Series.
F2808.2.D45   1998b   98–3217
982—dc21

Manufactured in the United States of America
1 2 3 4 5 6 – JR – 03 02 01 00 99 98

Contents

BOLIVIA

PARAGUAY

Iguazú
Falls

BRAZIL

A N D E S

Tucumán

A R G E N T I N A

C H I L E

URUGUAY

Buenos
Aires

Río de la Plata

PAMPAS

Mar del
Plata

ATLANTIC
OCEAN

P A T A G O N I A

Bariloche

A N D E S

PACIFIC OCEAN

Moreno
Glacier

N

TIERRA
DEL
FUEGO

mountains
plains
plateau
Lake
District

Miles

0   100   200   300   400

0   200   400   600

Kilometers

Welcome!

¡Hola! That means
"hello" in Spanish—
Argentina's main

The Moreno Glacier is a giant sheet of ice that covers 60 square miles of land in southern Patagonia.

language. Argentina takes up most of the southern part of the **continent** of South America. It has many neighbors. To the west lies Chile. Bolivia, Paraguay, Brazil, and Uruguay all sit to the north. Argentina's biggest neighbor is to the east—the Atlantic Ocean.

Map Whiz Quiz

Trace the outline of Argentina on a piece of paper. Write a "W" for west in Chile. At the country's tip, put an "S" for south. Put an "E" for east in the Atlantic Ocean. Go back up again to Paraguay, where you can write an "N" for north. Color in the Andes mountains on the border with Chile.

The rocky Andes (far left) make life difficult for the people who live there (left). In Tucumán (above), which is also called the Garden of the Nation, many types of tropical plants grow.

Going Up?

Argentina has different **landforms.** The biggest is the Andes **mountain range.** This long chain of mountains runs through

From a platform, tourists watch the rushing waters of Iguazú Falls on the border with Brazil.

South America, from Panama in the north to the southern tip of Argentina. The Andes act like an umbrella, keeping rain off the eastern slopes. But one spot, called Tucumán, in northern Argentina gets lots of rain.

¡Hola!

Today we visited Iguazú Falls. I have never seen anything like it! It is really 270 waterfalls rolled into one. We walked on a bridge to see them up close. All that rushing water made me feel dizzy. I'll be home soon!

People and Places

Flat fields called the **pampas** cover more than half of Argentina. Most Argentines live here. Wheat and corn grow well in the rich soil. Cows and sheep have plenty of grass to eat. Patagonia is just the opposite. The land is dry and rocky, and the weather is cold.

Only about one million people live in Patagonia. That's not many—Buenos Aires has 11 million people in one city!

The land to the south of Patagonia is Tierra del Fuego. Early explorers saw campfires burning on the shore. They named the area Tierra del Fuego, or "Land of Fire."

The Lake District in Patagonia

Few people live in Patagonia. Those who do raise sheep for their meat and wool.

Sheep munch on the tender grasses of the pampas.

9

The widest street in the world runs through Buenos Aires. It is called Avenida 9 de Julio, or July 9 Avenue.

Big City

Look at the map on page 4. Point to where the Río de la Plata meets the Atlantic Ocean. You have found Buenos Aires—Argentina's largest city. More than 11 million people live there! Buenos Aires has a busy **port** that ships from around the world visit. The ships

Pretty in Pink

Can you name the building in which the president of the United States works and lives? The White House, right? Well, in Argentina the building where the president works is called Casa Rosada. That means "pink house." Can you guess why?

carry goods to and from Argentina. The people who live in Buenos Aires are nicknamed *porteños*, or "port people."

On the Go

Bikes! Cars! Buses! There are lots of ways to get around in Argentina's cities. Traffic jams clog the streets, so many people would rather take a bus or a taxi—even if they own a car. A good, fast way to travel is by an underground train called a **subway.**

Traffic stands still on the Avenida 9 de Julio.

Subte, the Buenos Aires subway system, surfaces at a few stops around town.

In small towns, people ride horses, pedal bicycles, or drive cars.

Buses whisk people from place to place. That means fewer cars on the roads.

Los Indios

Thousands of years ago, *los indios* (Indians) lived in Argentina's mountains and plains. Each group had its own language and way of life.

Ancestors, or relatives, of modern-day Indians are long gone. But they left clay pots and stone weapons to remind us of the past.

14

Then the Spanish came to Argentina 400 years ago. They fought the Indians for land. Many Indians were killed in war or died of sicknesses. The rest were forced to work for the Spanish. Some moved to the mountains, where their great-great-great-grandchildren still live.

Cave of Hands

Early Indians left behind clues about how they lived. Some caves in Argentina have paintings that show dancing or hunting scenes. Other caves have handprints and footprints. Can you guess what decorates the walls in La Cueva de las Manos (Cave of Hands)?

Newspapers come in
many different languages.

An Italian man

Women from the
country of Yemen

Speak to Me

People from all over the world make
Argentina their home. Argentines include
folks from the countries of Spain, Italy,

Germany, and Poland, just to name a few. At home they probably speak the language of their old country. But in schools, stores, and offices, everybody speaks Spanish.

Gypsy Life

One group of Argentines—the Gypsies—lives in small bands that travel from town to town. They usually stay away from other people, except when they go to town to buy food or to sell goods.

A movable Gypsy tent

Español

As you know, Argentines speak *español*, or Spanish. In Spanish, some letters have different sounds than you might think. For example, the letter *j* sounds like *h*. Say the name Julia (HOO-lee-ah). But the letter *h* has

What could be more fun than talking with good friends?

The Spanish alphabet has 29 letters, three more than the English alphabet has. The double l (ll) makes a *ZSHE* sound, as in treasure. Say español. The ñ sounds like *NYEH* in onion. The double r (rr) in *burro* sounds like a stick dragged along a picket fence.

no sound at all. The word *hola* (meaning "hello") sounds like OH-lah.

The Plaza de Mayo, or May Plaza, in Buenos Aires is a popular spot to meet.

¡Hola!

Try saying these words:

good-bye	*chau*	(CHOW)
pleased to meet you	*mucho gusto*	(MOO-choh GOO-stoh)
yes	*sí*	(SEE)
no	*no*	(NOH)
see you later	*hasta luego*	(AH-stah loo-WAY-goh)

19

Two Argentine boys share a snack with their grandparents.

La Familia

La familia is Spanish for "the family." An Argentine family has a mother, a father, sisters, and brothers. Grandparents, aunts, or uncles may live in the same house, too. Many children also have godparents. Godparents could be family members or close friends. They help raise children by cheering them on at sports events, giving them gifts, or just being there to talk.

All in the Family

Here are the Spanish names for family members.

grandfather	*abuelo*	(ah-BWAY-loh)
grandmother	*abuela*	(ah-BWAY-lah)
father	*padre*	(PAH-dray)
mother	*madre*	(MAH-dray)
uncle	*tío*	(TEE-oh)
aunt	*tía*	(TEE-ah)
son	*hijo*	(EE-hoh)
daughter	*hija*	(EE-hah)
brother	*hermano*	(ehr-MAH-noh)
sister	*hermana*	(ehr-MAH-nah)

Kids who live in high-rise apartment buildings (left) *have lots of neighbors.* (Facing page) *On a nice day, it is fun to play at a local park.*

Day after Day

If you were from Argentina, what would life be like? City families have homes in high-rise apartment buildings. Kids meet friends after school to play soccer. Or they might take tennis lessons. City kids have chores, too. Country families live on **ranches,** and kids

Nap Time

Everyday, from 12 o'clock until 3 o'clock, Argentines take naps . . . or at least they rest. Everything stops. Schools and stores close. Then shops reopen and stay open until 7 o'clock.

spend much of their time outdoors. Young children may learn to ride horses. They help out on the family farm.

How would you like to have a horse to help you do your chores?

23

School

Brrrring! There is the bell—time for school. Preschoolers line up in the schoolyard like a centipede (a bug with 100 legs). Each puts his or her hands on the hips of the child in

These kids all go to the same school. They wear matching aprons, called guardapolvos, which means "keep off the dust."

A Geography Lesson

Argentine kids go to school while you are on summer vacation. Why? Argentina is in the **Southern Hemisphere** because the country is below the **equator**. This imaginary line divides the world in half. In the Southern Hemisphere, the seasons are opposite the ones in the **Northern Hemisphere,** where the United States is located. In Argentina summer falls in December, while winter comes in July.

Argentine students only go to school for half a day. Some kids go in the morning, while others go in the afternoon.

front, and they march in a long line. After they are inside, the kids put on their *guardapolvos,* or aprons, to keep their clothes clean during the day.

Sports

Diego Maradona

Heads up! Soccer is a favorite sport among Argentines of all ages.

What is the number-one sport in Argentina? *¡Fútbol!* Fútbol is the Spanish word for soccer. Almost any day, you can find a game happening on television or at a local park. One of the world's most famous soccer players, Diego Maradona, is from

Playing with Horses

Horses play a big part in Argentina's history. They are used to travel almost anywhere, especially on the huge pampas. Argentine cowboys made up a game to play on horseback. It is called *pato*. To play pato, two teams of riders on horseback pass a ball. A team can score by putting the ball through a net like a basketball hoop.

Argentina. Other sports popular in Argentina include tennis, skiing, horse racing, car racing, and boxing.

Gabriela Sabatini, an Argentine tennis star, won many titles in the late 1980s and early 1990s.

Taking It Easy

Kids everywhere like to have fun, right? In Argentina they ride bikes, build go-carts, and watch their favorite TV shows. During the summer, kids splash in the local swimming pool or relax at a nearby beach. Many kids meet friends for a soccer game.

One thing that you find no matter where in the world you live is friendship. These Argentine kids meet after school.

Whether on horseback, on roller skates, or just goofing around, kids everywhere know how to have fun.

Others would rather roller-skate. In the country, children horse around— on horses!

There are fun things to do in Argentina all year. In the summer, take a dip in the ocean near Mar del Plata. In the winter, bring your skis to Las Leñas ski area.

Take a Trip

When Argentines want to get away, they have plenty of great places to choose from. They may visit family members or go shopping. Other folks head for the ocean off the coast of Mar del Plata.

Bariloche is famous for its chocolate.

A huge clock tower stands in Bariloche's main plaza. Every day at noon, the clock rings. Four wooden statues come out of the clock tower and turn as the clock strikes 12 times.

The city of Bariloche in the Lake District of Patagonia provides a cool getaway. It was built to look like a town in Germany.

31

Argentine men wear clothes that the gauchos wore, including baggy pants, called bombachas.

Ride 'em, Cowboy

An Argentine cowboy is called a gaucho. Years ago gauchos worked on the pampas, watching over herds of cattle and living off the land. True gauchos do not exist anymore, but

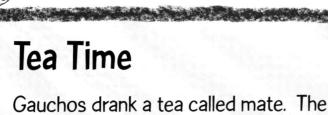

Tea Time

Gauchos drank a tea called mate. The people of Argentina drink it almost everyday. To make mate, they pour boiling water over yerba mate (crushed tea leaves). After it cools, they sip the tea through a *bombilla*—a metal straw with a bulb at the end that takes out the leaves.

Argentines hold parades and **rodeos** in memory of the gaucho lifestyle. A rodeo is an event that includes contests on horseback.

People who live in the country often continue the gaucho way of life.

33

Song and Dance

Some kinds of music and dance in Argentina give a history lesson. One dance, *el escondido*, tells a story of a gaucho who must hide from his enemies. Musicians play the accordion-like *bandoneón*, while dancers clap their hands and stomp their feet to keep time to the beat.

A group of dancers wearing old-time clothes performs a gaucho dance for an audience.

Musicians play a bandoneón *and a guitar* (left) *and the* zampoñas, *or panpipes* (above).

Dance with Me

A sad type of dance and music called the tango comes from Argentina. Tango dancers learn hard steps and hand movements. Like gaucho music, many tangos are played on the bandoneón.

Picture Perfect

Where can you find art in Argentina? In La Boca, a neighborhood in Buenos Aires. The artists who live there have covered the

The buildings in La Boca neighborhood in Buenos Aires are painted with the colors of the rainbow.

Florencio Molina Campos (1891–1959) painted pictures of gaucho life. He is also known for his beautiful images of the pampas. His style looked like cartoons and earned him a job with the Walt Disney Studios in Hollywood, California.

Colorful wall paintings brighten up the streets.

buildings with bright colors. The wall paintings, called **murals,** in El Caminito are huge.

Argentines eat more beef than people anywhere else in the world.

Grill It!

Beef is the most popular food in Argentina. Argentines like to **barbecue,** or grill, beef over an open fire. They also barbecue pork, lamb, fish, chicken, and turkey.

There is no such thing as a one-stop grocery store in Argentina. Most Argentines shop at markets for fresh fruit and vegetables, at butcher shops for fresh meat, and at bakeries for fresh bread. One kind of store, called a *galletitería*, sells only crackers and cookies.

A waiter serves up a plate of ñoquis—pasta made from potato dough.

Italian foods, like ravioli, spaghetti, and lasagna, are very popular in Argentina. And gnocchi is Italian for ñoquis.

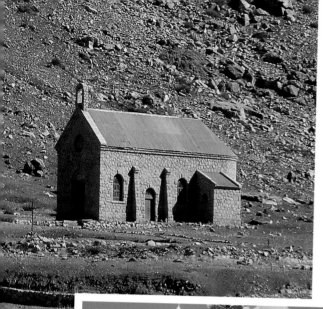

Holy Days

Most Argentines belong to the Roman Catholic Church. In fact, many towns even have their own saint (holy person). Once a year, townspeople hold celebrations to honor the saint.

A Catholic church in Patagonia (top) *stands alone. A parade* (left) *is one way townspeople celebrate their saint.*

Members of a Catholic church leave after a Sunday service.

Another important religious holiday is Christmas. Instead of Santa Claus, Papá Noel brings gifts. But children really look forward to Three Kings' Day on January 6. Christians believe three kings gave gifts to the baby Jesus on this day. Children leave their shoes outside so the kings will leave them gifts, too.

Celebrate!

Argentines also celebrate their country and their culture. During the festival of Vendimia—the grape festival—people praise the rich earth that helps the grapes to grow. Argentines honor the majestic mountains during the Snow Festival in Barlioche.

A grape grower from Mendoza proudly shows off his crop.

And do not forget about the sea! In the first week of December, the townspeople of Mar del Plata party during the National Sea Festival.

Let's Dance

Carlos Gardel

The tango is danced in countries all around the world. But one Argentine town near Buenos Aires holds its own Tango Festival. The festival takes place in the first two weeks of January. Carlos Gardel is a famous tango musician. Although he died many years ago, he is still the king of the tango, much like Elvis Presley is known as the "King of Rock and Roll."

Colorful umbrellas dot the beaches of Mar del Plata.

New Words to Learn

barbecue: A way of cooking meat or fish over an open flame or on hot coals.

continent: Any one of seven large areas of land. The continents are Africa, Antarctica, Asia, Australia, Europe, North America, and South America.

equator: An imaginary line that circles a globe at the middle, dividing the world into a north half and a south half.

landform: A natural feature, such as a mountain or a plain.

mountain range: A series, or group, of mountains—the parts of the earth's surface that rise high into the sky.

mural: A large-scale work of art painted directly on a wall.

Northern Hemisphere: One half of the earth's surface that lies above the equator. The United States is in the Northern Hemisphere.

pampa: A large area of flat land covered by grass. The

This house lies in Ushuaia, the southernmost town in the world!

pampas are located in South America, east of the Andes.

port: A safe area on the shore of a body of water where ships can load and unload goods.

ranch: A large farm for raising cattle, sheep, or horses.

rodeo: A contest usually performed on horseback. Rodeo events include calf roping and bull riding.

Southern Hemisphere: One half of the earth's surface that lies below the equator. Argentina is in the Southern Hemisphere.

subway: An underground train that moves large numbers of people quickly.

45

New Words to Say

bandoneón	bahn-doh-nay-OHN
Bariloche	bah-ree-LOH-chay
Buenos Aires	BWAY-nohs EYE-rays
Diego Maradona	dee-AY-goh mah-rah-DOH-nah
escondido	ehs-cohn-DEE-doh
escuela	ehs-KWAY-lah
español	ehs-pah-NYOHL
familia	fah-MEE-lee-ah
fútbol	FOOT-bohl
galletitería	gah-zhe-tee-teh-REE-ah
gaucho	GOW-choh
guardapolvos	gwahr-dah-POHL-vohs
Iguazú Falls	ee-gwah-SOO FAHLS
Papá Noel	pah-PAH noh-EHL
porteños	pohr-TAY- nyohs
quena	KAY-nah
Río de la Plata	REE-oh day lah PLAH-tah
Tucumán	too-koo-MAHN
zampoñas	sahm-POH-nyahs

More Books to Read

Belleville, Cheryl Walsh. *Rodeo.* Minneapolis: Carolrhoda Books, 1985.

Brusca, Maria Cristina. *My Mama's Little Ranch on the Pampas.* New York: Henry Holt and Company, Inc., 1994.

Brusca, Maria Cristina. *On the Pampas.* New York: Henry Holt and Company, Inc., 1991.

Jacobsen, Karen. *A New True Book: Argentina.* Chicago: Children's Press, Inc., 1990.

Parnell, Helga. *Cooking the South American Way.* Minneapolis, Lerner Publications Company, 1991.

New Words to Find